TOMASO ALBINONI

Oboe Concerto in B♭ Major, C...

Oboe Concerto in D Major, Op. 7, No. ...

Oboe Concerto in D Minor, Op. 9, No. 2

PLAYBACK+

Speed • Pitch • Balance • Loop

To access audio visit:
www.halleonard.com/mylibrary

7179-1886-2704-3916

ISBN: 978-1-59615-347-9

Music Minus One

EXCLUSIVELY DISTRIBUTED BY

HAL•LEONARD®

Visit Hal Leonard Online at
www.halleonard.com

Contact Us:
Hal Leonard
7777 West Bluemound Road
Milwaukee, WI 53213
Email: info@halleonard.com

In Europe contact:
Hal Leonard Europe Limited
42 Wigmore Street
Marylebone, London, W1U 2RN
Email: info@halleonardeurope.com

In Australia contact:
Hal Leonard Australia Pty. Ltd.
4 Lentara Court
Cheltenham, Victoria, 3192 Australia
Email: info@halleonard.com.au

Contents

This edition has been prepared from original sources. Phrasing, ornamentation, and dynamics are mostly left to the discretion of the performer as they were in the 18th century. To blend best with the orchestral performance, it is advised to emulate the phrasing and dynamics of the soloist on the complete performance include.

Movements often start with an orchestral tutti which the soloist can also play at his or her discretion.

4

Albinoni – Concerto in B♭, Op 7 No 3

58

61

64

68

Taps:

Adagio   **2**

8

15

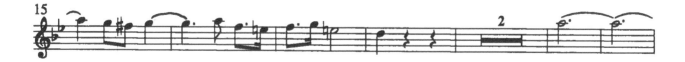

23

27

32

6

Taps:

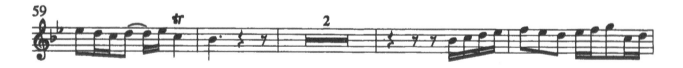

Albinoni – Concerto in D, Op 7 No 6

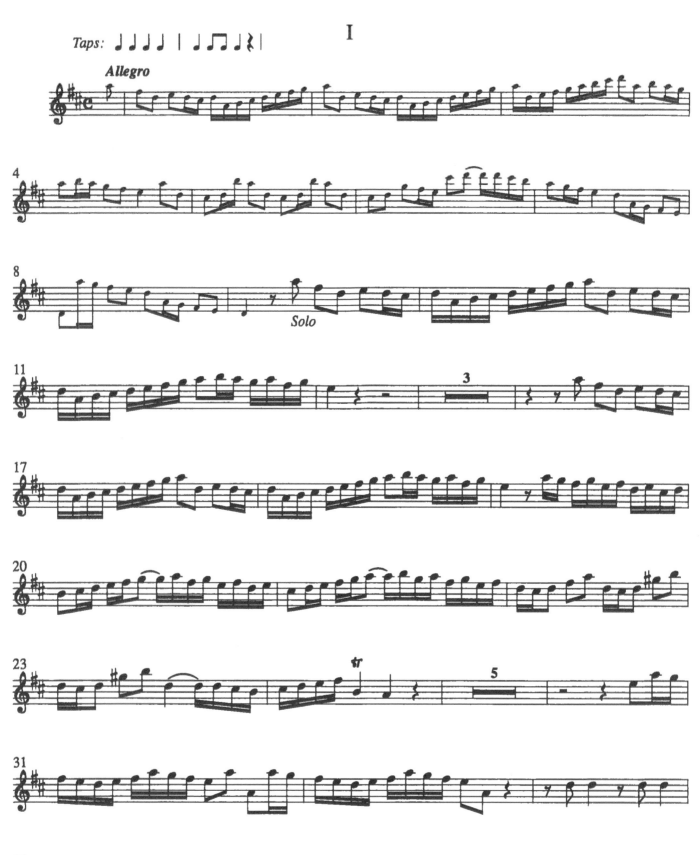

Taps:

II

Taps:

III

I

Albinoni – Concerto in D Minor, Op 9 No 2

68

72

77

88

94

124

130

136

141

148

152

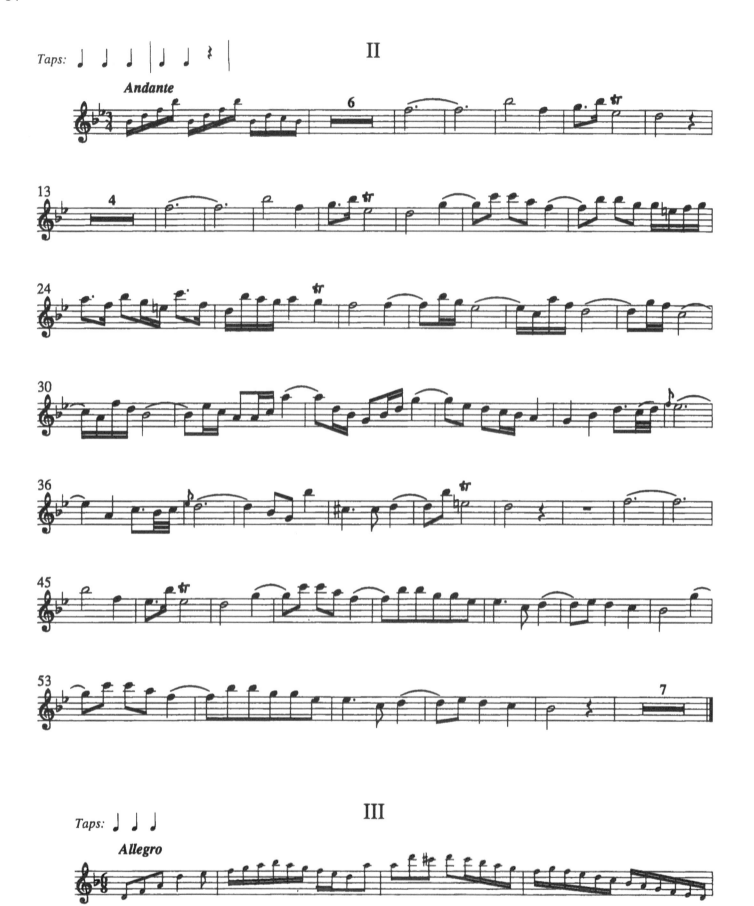